SHORT WALKS RIBBLE VALLEY

by Mark Sutcliffe

The whaleback of Pendle stretches out from the bridleway above Sabden (Walk 7)

CONTENTS

Using this guide.. 4
Route summary table 6
Map key... 7
Introduction.. 9
   Walking in the Ribble Valley 10
   A delicious walking destination.. 10
   Bases... 10
   Travel 11
   When to visit 11

The walks

1.	Roman Ribchester...	13
2.	Longridge Fell	19
3.	Dinckley and Marles Wood	23
4.	The Tolkien Trail	29
5.	Dean Clough Reservoir...	35
6.	Spring Wood and Whalley Nab	41
7.	Wiswell, Portfield Bar and the Nick of Pendle.............	47
8.	The easy way up Pendle...	53
9.	Clitheroe Castle and the River Ribble..........................	59
10.	Waddington village circular	65
11.	Waddington and Bashall Eaves from Edisford	69
12.	The foothills of Pendle from Downham	75
13.	Grindleton Fell and the pine woods	79
14.	Sawley and Bolton-by-Bowland	83
15.	Sawley to Clitheroe along the Ribble Way	89

Useful information... 95

USING THIS GUIDE

Routes in this book

In this book you will find a selection of easy or moderate walks suitable for almost everyone, including casual walkers and families with children, or for when you only have a short time to fill. The routes have been carefully chosen to allow you to explore the area and its attractions. Most routes are circular or out-and-back, although some linear walks may be included that use public transport to get back to the start. Although there may be some climbs there is no challenging terrain, but do bear in mind that conditions can sometimes be wet or muddy underfoot. A route summary table is included on page 6 to help you choose the right walk.

Clothing and footwear

You won't need any special equipment to enjoy these walks. The weather in Britain can be changeable, so choose clothing suitable for the season and wear or carry a waterproof jacket. For footwear, comfortable walking boots or trainers with a good grip are best. A small rucksack for drinks, snacks and spare clothing is useful. See www.adventuresmart.uk.

Walk descriptions

At the beginning of each walk you'll find all the information you need:

- start/finish location, with a what3words address to help you find it
- parking and transport information, estimated walking time, total distance and climb
- details of public toilets available along the route and where you can get refreshments
- a summary of the key highlights of the walk and what you might see

Timings given are the time to complete the walk at a reasonable walking pace. Allow extra time for extended stops or if walking with children.

The route is described in clear, easy-to-follow directions, with each waypoint marked on an accompanying map extract. It's a good idea to read the whole of the route instructions before setting out, so that you know what to expect.

Maps, GPX files and what3words

Extracts from the OS® 1:25,000 map accompany each route. GPX files for all the walks in this book are available to download at www.cicerone.co.uk/1236/gpx.

What3words is a free smartphone app which identifies every 3m square of the globe with a unique three-word address, e.g. ///destiny.cafe.sonic. For more information see https://what3words.com/products/what3words-app.

USING THIS GUIDE

Walking with children

Even young children can be surprisingly strong walkers, but every family is different and you may need to adapt the timings given in this book to take that into account. Make sure you go at the pace of the slowest member and choose a walk with an exciting objective in mind, such as a cave, river, waterfall or picnic spot. Many of the walks can be shortened to suit – suggestions are included at the end of the route description.

Dogs

Sheep or cattle may be found grazing on a number of these walks. Keep dogs under control at all times so that they don't scare or disturb livestock or wildlife. Cattle, particularly cows with calves, may very occasionally pose a risk to walkers with dogs. If you ever feel threatened by cattle, you should let go of your dog's lead and let it run free.

Enjoying the countryside responsibly

Enjoy the countryside and treat it with respect to protect our natural environments. Stick to footpaths and take your litter home with you. When driving, slow down on rural roads and park considerately, or better still use public transport. For more details check out www.gov.uk/countryside-code.

The Countryside Code

Respect everyone
- be considerate to those living in, working in and enjoying the countryside
- leave gates and property as you find them
- do not block access to gateways or driveways when parking
- be nice, say hello, share the space
- follow local signs and keep to marked paths unless wider access is available

Protect the environment
- take your litter home – leave no trace of your visit
- do not light fires and only have BBQs where signs say you can
- always keep dogs under control and in sight
- dog poo – bag it and bin it – any public waste bin will do
- care for nature – do not cause damage or disturbance

Enjoy the outdoors
- check your route and local conditions
- plan your adventure – know what to expect and what you can do
- enjoy your visit, have fun, make a memory

ROUTE SUMMARY TABLE

WALK NAME	START POINT	TIME	DISTANCE
1. Roman Ribchester	Ribchester	2¾hr	10.5km (6½ miles)
2. Longridge Fell	Viewpoint on Old Clitheroe Road	2hr	6km (3¾ miles)
3. Dinckley and Marles Wood	Old Langho	2hr	7km (4¼ miles)
4. The Tolkien Trail	Hurst Green	2¾hr	10.5km (6½ miles)
5. Dean Clough Reservoir	Langho railway station	2hr	7km (4¼ miles)
6. Spring Wood and Whalley Nab	Spring Wood, Whalley	2½hr	8km (5 miles)
7. Wiswell, Portfield Bar and the Nick of Pendle	Wiswell	2½hr	8km (5 miles)
8. The easy way up Pendle	Nick of Pendle	3hr	11km (6¾ miles)
9. Clitheroe Castle and the River Ribble	Clitheroe railway station	2hr	6.5km (4 miles)
10. Waddington village circular	Waddington	2hr	7km (4¼ miles)
11. Waddington and Bashall Eaves from Edisford	Edisford Road car park, Clitheroe	2¾hr	9km (5½ miles)
12. The foothills of Pendle from Downham	Downham	2½hr	8km (5 miles)
13. Grindleton Fell and the pine woods	Grindleton	3¼hr	10km (6¼ miles)
14. Sawley and Bolton-by-Bowland	Sawley	2½hr	9.5km (6 miles)
15. Sawley to Clitheroe along the Ribble Way	Sawley	2½hr	9km (5½ miles)

ROUTE SUMMARY TABLE

HIGHLIGHTS
Roman museum and bath house, River Ribble
Stunning views, wildlife, woodland
River Ribble, woodlands, pub
Historic and literary links, woodlands, river walk
Wainwright associations, views, accessible by rail
Woodland, views, industrial heritage, accessible by rail
Views, folklore, ancient history, gastropub
Views, folklore and history
History, River Ribble wildlife, accessible by rail
Scenic village, woodland, wildlife, pubs
Scenic villages, history, pubs
Views, scenic village, TV and film links, pub
Views, pine forests, gastropub
History, River Ribble, wildlife, gastropub
Sawley Abbey, River Ribble, sculpture trail

SYMBOLS USED ON ROUTE MAPS

- **S** Start point
- **F** Finish point
- **SF** Start and finish at the same place
- **4** Waypoint
- ∿ Route line

MAPPING IS SHOWN AT A SCALE OF 1:25,000

0 KM — 0.25 — 0.5
0 miles — 0.25

DOWNLOAD THE GPX FILES FOR FREE AT
www.cicerone.co.uk/1236/gpx

Wild garlic carpets the banks of a tributary stream (Walk 6)

INTRODUCTION

The River Ribble from Dinckley suspension bridge (Walk 3)

The Ribble Valley is a genuine walker's paradise. This unspoiled corner of rural East Lancashire has it all: gentle rolling countryside, wooded river valleys and some more challenging hill walks for those with an appetite for adventure.

These stunning landscapes are criss-crossed with footpaths and bridleways and there's a huge selection of circular walks – ranging from riverside rambles and gentle afternoon ambles through scenic villages, to challenging mini-mountains like famous Pendle Hill, offering stunning views for the more energetically inclined.

While the Ribble Valley extends from the Yorkshire Dales, where the river rises on the fells above the iconic Ribblehead Viaduct, to the Lancashire coast at Lytham, this guide focuses on the varied scenery around the middle reaches of the river.

Here, the Ribble flows through fertile pastureland and wooded valley where visitors can expect to see kingfishers, dippers, egrets, goosanders and the occasional passing osprey. Among the woodland and hedgerows expect to see rarities such as pied flycatchers and redstarts, while in the uplands, look out for hen harrier, merlin and ring ouzel.

At the heart of this verdant pastoral landscape is the bustling market town of Clitheroe – surrounded by a

SHORT WALKS RIBBLE VALLEY

cluster of picture-postcard villages like Waddington, Downham, Hurst Green and Bolton-by-Bowland. Larger settlements like Whalley, Ribchester and Longridge have their own charm and history and are also worthy of exploration.

Walking in the Ribble Valley

This collection of leisurely walks visits towns and villages which usually have some interesting historical, natural, or cultural significance. The walking is generally easy and undemanding, with the occasional steeper incline or descent, but the Ribble Valley does get a lot of rain throughout the year and sections of some routes will become muddy – especially in winter.

All walks are circular, with the exception of Walk 15, and under 11km (6¾ miles) in length with less than 300m of climbing. Apart from the challenge route (Walk 13) they can be comfortably completed in 2½ to 3hr. Many of the walks will also pass a welcoming country inn which welcomes walkers for refreshments.

A delicious walking destination

After working up a healthy appetite amid the stunning scenery of the Ribble Valley, what better way to reward your exertions than with an indulgent meal at one of the region's

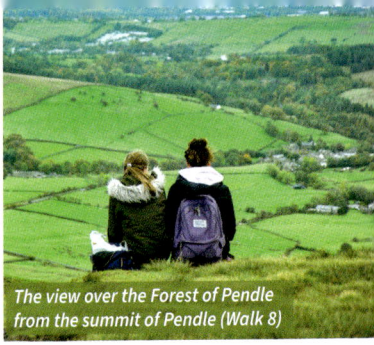

The view over the Forest of Pendle from the summit of Pendle (Walk 8)

many gastropubs and characterful country inns?

Events like the annual Clitheroe Food Festival have really put the area on the foodie map of Britain and the Ribble Valley is establishing a deserved reputation for offering walkers a warm Lancastrian welcome and serving up distinctive dishes reflecting the very best local produce.

The valley's bustling market towns and picturesque villages are home to some of the best gastropubs in Britain, with outstanding eateries like the Freemason's Arms in Wiswell, the Higher Buck in Waddington or the Rum Fox in Grindleton all highly recommended.

Bases

For those who would like to linger longer and explore this enchanting corner of Lancashire in greater depth, many of the country inns and boutique hotels also offer comfortable accommodation. Clitheroe has a number of hotels and guesthouses and its

WHEN TO VISIT

charming town centre is characterised by independent retailers and a vibrant market, while an excellent Camping and Caravanning Club site is located at Edisford – right beside the Ribble on the edge of town.

The Waddington Arms in Waddington and the Assheton Arms in Downham offer comfortable village accommodation and there is a good choice of holiday cottages throughout the Ribble Valley available through the usual online platforms.

Travel

By road, the Ribble Valley can be reached via junction 31 on the M6, following the A59 eastbound to Clitheroe. By rail, Clitheroe is just over an hour's journey from Manchester on a direct train from Manchester Victoria. From the West Coast Mainline, there's an hourly service from Preston to Clitheroe, changing at Blackburn.

The 280 bus connects Preston and Skipton, calling at Clitheroe en route. Public transport is patchy in the Ribble Valley, but services 66, 67, 11, 5, 5A and 11 connect with the villages where our walks start via Clitheroe Interchange.

When to visit

The Ribble Valley climate is generally mild and somewhat damp, although snow occasionally dusts the tops of the higher summits in winter. Late spring is a glorious time to visit and admire the wildflowers in the meadows, and while tourists are beginning to discover this area, the summer months are not generally too busy. Early autumn is another ideal time to visit, when the footpaths are at their driest and the riverside woodland melts into a blaze of autumn colour mirroring the roaring log fires found in the valley's welcoming country inns.

The 'Big End' of Pendle from the terrace of the Assheton Arms, Downham (Walk 12)

The riverside woodlands are carpeted with bluebells and ransoms in spring

WALK 1
Roman Ribchester

Start/finish	*The White Bull, Ribchester*
Locate	*///commended.panning.newest*
Cafes/pubs	*Pubs and cafes in Ribchester*
Transport	*Bus service 45 from Blackburn to Preston*
Parking	*Church St pay-and-display car park (PR3 3ZH)*
Toilets	*In car park*

Time 2¾hr
Distance 10.5km (6½ miles)
Climb 100m

A riverside ramble through the woods alongside the Ribble from the historic Roman garrison town of Ribchester

Ribchester is a charming village with a rich history dating back to Roman times. This walk starts in the heart of the village, passing the Roman Museum and Bath House before following the Ribble through deciduous woodland and over an elegant footbridge. Although the walk is largely flat, it's one of the more challenging walks in this book, so take a selection of drinks and snacks to keep you going and consider wearing wellies in spring or autumn as some sections can be muddy.

Ribchester Roman Museum

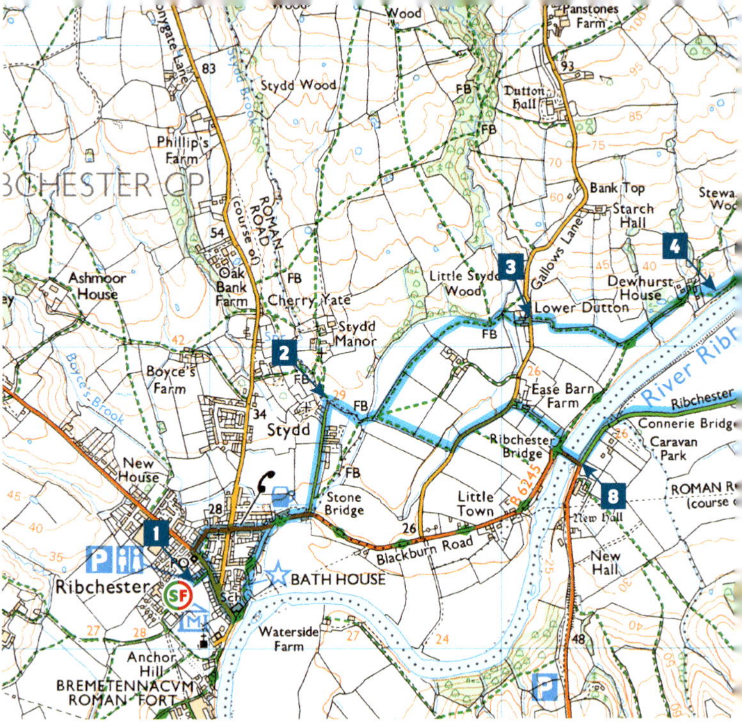

The White Bull's distinctive frontage

1 From the White Bull pub walk to the riverside, where you'll find the Roman Museum. Turn left, heading upstream on a riverside footpath past the **Roman Bath House** and war memorial to join the road. Head right, following the road past the Ribchester Arms, then left along Stydd Lane to the church.

> It is worth a quick detour to explore the Roman Bath House. The building dates to around AD100 and its foundations are clearly visible and well preserved.

2 After the church, where the track crosses a stream, turn right and follow the field boundary to cross the

footbridge then follow the path left over the fields to reach the stream, then veer right and through the farmyard to **Gallows Lane**.

3 Cross the road and continue over the fields, keeping the boundary hedge on your left and heading for two mature trees. Beyond the trees, veer slightly right and over a stile in the corner of the field near the barns to join a tarmac track. Continue left along the track to the farm then veer right to join the Ribble Way alongside the **River Ribble**.

4 Continue upstream into the woodlands, following the diversion left around an eroded section of footpath through the woods. Rejoin the path at the footbridge, cross and continue through **Haugh Wood**.

5 At the edge of the woodland, follow the footpath left through a kissing gate and into a field. Climb along the edge of the wood then across the field and through a gate. Veer half left, climbing slightly, then go through a gate/stile across the paddock and through kissing gates either side of the track.

The River Ribble at Ribchester

6 Continue across the left-hand field boundary and over a footbridge in the corner of the field then climb steadily along the right-hand boundary of the next field. Go over a stile in the corner of the field and continue straight on along the field boundary of the next two fields, then through a metal gate to join a track. After 50m turn hard left along a path to a footbridge.

7 Cross the footbridge and on the far side head right, following the river downstream. The next section is often muddy, so tread carefully. Continue through **Marles Wood**, following the Ribble Valley Jubilee Trail to the edge of woodland. Fork right and over the

> ⓘ *The imposing portico of the 18th-century White Bull Inn at the centre of Ribchester is constructed from Roman columns which were recovered from the River Ribble.*

footbridge then follow the path up to join the road. Head right down the hill and follow the road past **Salesbury Hall**. Continue for 1.2km to reach the bridge.

8 Cross **Ribchester Bridge** and at the far side head right along a track for 50m, then left across fields to reach a

WALK 1 – ROMAN RIBCHESTER

road. Turn left along the road then, after 150m, take the footpath on the right across the field to a footbridge. Cross the footbridge and follow the field boundary to reach the track that leads onto Stydd Lane. Return to the main road, then turn right past the Ribchester Arms and continue along Ribchester Road then left into Church Street to return to the White Bull.

> **— To shorten**
> At Waypoint 8 cross Ribchester Bridge and walk along the footpath alongside Blackburn Road into Ribchester. This shortens the route by 600m but beware of the traffic, which tends to travel quite quickly along this road.

A legion of Roman artefacts

Back in the 1st century, the Ribble was navigable by larger craft as far upstream as Ribchester, and the Romans established a riverside wharfe and garrison fort here which operated between 72CE and 373CE. As well as direct access to the sea, the fort was strategically located at the junction of two Roman roads running north–south and east–west. The Roman Museum is open daily (admission £4) and chronicles the history of Ribchester or Bremetenacum as it was known in Roman times. A series of archaeological excavations have unearthed a rich seam of artefacts offering a unique insight into the strategic importance of this location to the defence of Northern Britannia (https://ribchestermuseum.org).

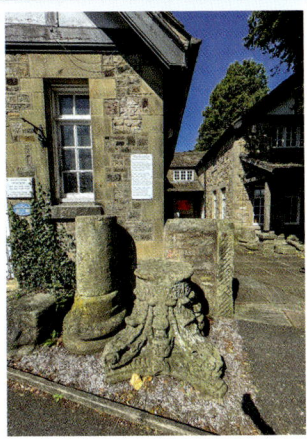

Ornate Roman stonemasonry outside Ribchester Roman Museum

The footbridge over the Brownslow Brook, which flows off Longridge fell

WALK 2
Longridge Fell

Start/finish	Layby at viewpoint near quarries on Old Clitheroe Road
Locate	///blown.barman.serious
Cafes/pubs	None on route
Transport	No public transport
Parking	Layby and viewpoint on Clitheroe Old Road (PR3 2YU)
Toilets	No public toilets on route

Time 2hr
Distance 6km (3¾ miles)
Climb 160m

Enjoy sublime views of the Ribble Valley and the Forest of Bowland on this rewarding walk through heather, bilberry and woodland

This delightful walk is the shortest in the collection, but punches well above its weight in terms of views and scenery. Making the steep ascent of Birdie Brow by car takes a few hundred feet of climbing out of the equation, leaving you to enjoy the expansive views over the Ribble Valley and Forest of Bowland. Look out for birds like goldcrests and crossbills in the plantations and you may see deer in the early morning or evening.

Looking north to the Bowland Fells from the summit ridge

SHORT WALKS RIBBLE VALLEY

1 From the layby at the viewpoint, head west along the lane past the edge of the woodland and after 500m take the footpath along a track on the right. Climb steadily along the track for another 500m to join a grassy footpath next to some rather ornate gates for **Moor Game Hall** and go straight on, heading towards the woods. Climb through the heather and bilberry to reach a gap in wall. The views open out to the west over the Lancashire coast and – on a clear day – right across Liverpool Bay to the mountains of Snowdonia.

2 Go through the gap and veer slightly right, continuing to climb to reach the forestry track and head left along a footpath running parallel to the track. Follow the path around the edge of the woods, heading right after 250m and continuing along the edge of the woods and over a wooden stile and then a stone stile. Head right alongside the wall for 400m to a metal kissing gate.

Straight ahead is the summit of Spire Hill, which is worth a short detour. The view from the

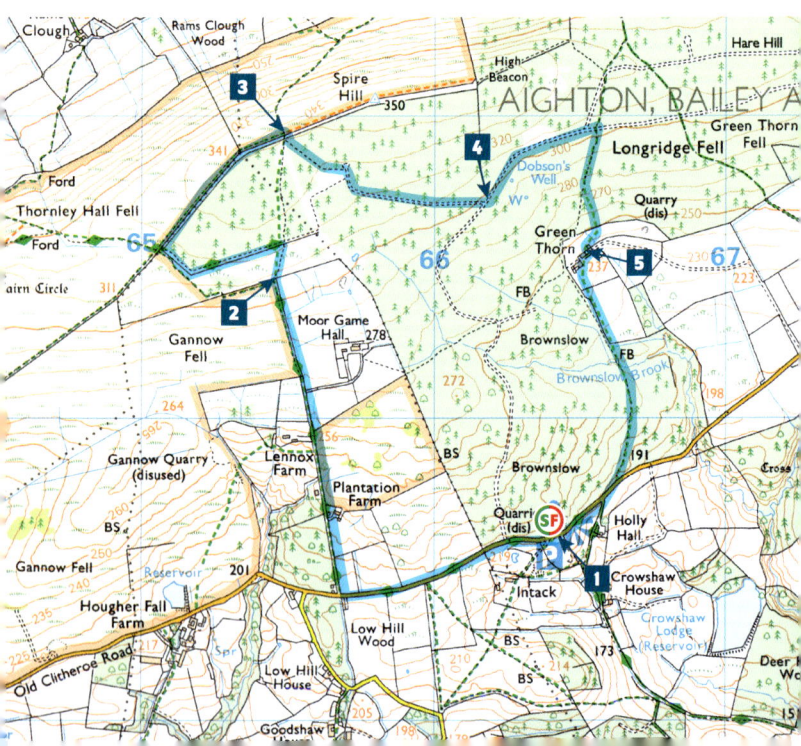

The summit trig point is just short diversion off the route

trig point is one of the finest in Lancashire, stretching from Blackpool Tower on the coast, across the Bowland Fells and over to the Three Peaks in Yorkshire.

3 Go through the kissing gate and veer left through trees to a clearing. Follow the track slightly right as it leaves the clearing then heads left, descending gently to a junction of forestry tracks.

4 At a junction, turn left along the track for 350m and after the track forks, take the grassy footpath on right. Descend through woods as the track becomes rockier to reach the buildings at **Green Thorn**.

5 Continue past the farm buildings. The path becomes less distinct in the dense pine woods, but continue descending steadily and cross the **Brownslow Brook** on the footbridge. Continue for another 300m to reach the road and then return to the layby on the footpath running parallel to the road.

> **− To shorten**
>
> At Waypoint 4, instead of heading left at the junction of forestry tracks, head right and follow the track through the woods for 1.3km to reach the road and the layby. This saves 500m (8min).

Fine deciduous woodland at Marles Wood

WALK 3
Dinckley and Marles Wood

Time 2hr
Distance 7km (4¼ miles)
Climb 100m

Start/finish	The Black Bull Inn, Old Langho
Locate	///robes.innovator.tells
Cafes/pubs	Pub in Old Langho
Transport	Bus service 25 from Blackburn or Clitheroe
Parking	On street
Toilets	No public toilets on route

A gentle amble through pastureland down to the River Ribble and a riverside walk through mature woodland before returning to a popular country inn

Downstream of Whalley, where the rivers Hodder and Calder merge with the main river, the Ribble becomes a wider, more powerful current. In the floods of 2015, the original suspension footbridge was all but destroyed by the swollen torrent following unprecedented rainfall. This walk visits the new bridge, before meandering downstream through Marles Wood to a large lagoon.

Marles Wood beside the River Ribble

1 Take the driveway next to the pub and follow it past the lodges and over the stile beside the gate into the field. Continue along the track, veering slightly left after 200m to follow a faint path towards the farm buildings. Descend to the footbridge and cross the stream.

> ⓘ *Rising above the iconic Ribblehead Viaduct in the Yorkshire Dales, the Ribble flows south into Lancashire before arcing west into the Irish Sea at Lytham – a distance of 121km (75 miles).*

WALK 3 – DINCKLEY AND MARLES WOOD

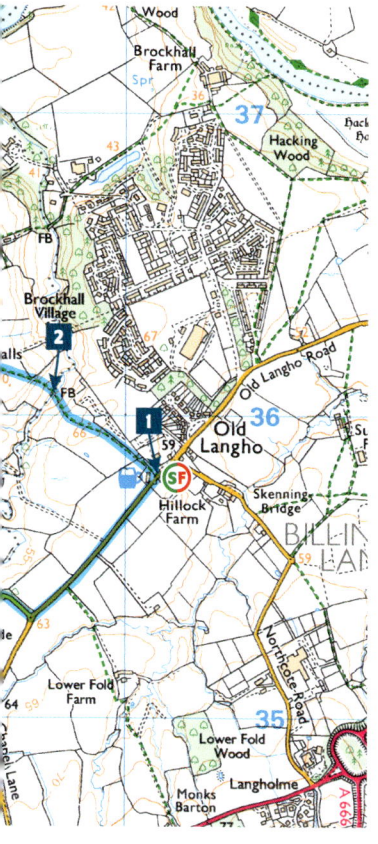

2 Climb straight up the other side of the valley, then, at the lip of the valley, head half left across the field towards the farmhouse. Continue through the metal gate beside the yellow marker post then straight on between the buildings and onto the lane.

3 Continue along the lane for 500m into the village of **Dinckley**. At the junction, turn right and follow the lane for 200m before joining a driveway. Continue down the driveway into the woodland, following it round to the left and descending through the gate to the river.

4 At the riverbank, turn left and follow the river downstream for 2.5km, passing the elegant new footbridge.

> The new bridge stands 1.5m higher than its predecessor, which was destroyed by the floods of 2015. Just downstream of the bridge, you'll find a stretch of sandy beach – perfect for a spot of sunbathing or a picnic.

Dinckley suspension bridge from the river beach

> ⓘ *The Ribble Valley Jubilee Trail is a 105km (65 mile) circular hiking route which was opened to commemorate Her Late Majesty Queen Elizabeth II's Platinum Jubilee.*

Continue along the river bank and into **Marles Wood** and after 700m, just after the rocks where the Ribble meanders right into a huge lagoon, take the footpath off to the left, climbing through the trees to reach a fork.

The Ribble narrows before forming a lagoon near Salesbury Hall

5 At the fork, take the path left and climb through the car park to meet the road. Keeping mindful of the traffic, head left and continue uphill along the lane, past Dinckley, for 2.5km to reach the bridge over **Dinckley Brook**.

6 After the bridge, at the junction, turn left and continue along the lane for 500m to reach the pub where you started.

Looking upstream from Lower Hodder Bridge

WALK 4
The Tolkien Trail

Start/finish	*Opposite the Shireburn Arms, Hurst Green*
Locate	*///retail.undivided.sadly*
Cafes/pubs	*Pubs and cafe in Hurst Green*
Transport	*Bus service 5 from Clitheroe Interchange*
Parking	*On street*
Toilets	*St Peter's Club*

Time 2¾hr
Distance 10.5km (6½ miles)
Climb 135m

A journey through 'The Shire' in the footsteps of JRR Tolkien, who stayed at nearby Stonyhurst College

The Tolkien Trail is one of the most popular short walks in Lancashire – and is consequently a busy route all year round. The walk follows the River Ribble and woodland tracks and passes Stonyhurst College. The fantasy writer JRR Tolkien is thought to have written significant portions of *The Lord of the Rings* while staying at Stonyhurst, where the rolling pastureland, woodlands and rivers inspired the landscapes of 'The Shire'.

Pendle Hill seen from near Stonyhurst College

Stonyhurst College

1 From the bus shelter opposite the pub, cross Avenue Road and continue past St Peter's Club along the lane past the houses and go through a gate onto the fields. Follow the left-hand field boundary and go through a gateway before turning right. Follow the fence across two more fields, descending to cross the stream and climbing beside the woodland to the boundary of **Stonyhurst College**.

As one of the leading Catholic boarding schools in England, Stonyhurst has many famous alumni – including Sir Arthur Conan Doyle and JRR Tolkien, who stayed at the college while his son John was studying there.

Go through the gate and turn right past the observatory, following the track downhill past **Hall Barn Farm**.

WALK 4 – THE TOLKIEN TRAIL

> ⓘ *Sir Arthur Conan Doyle named Sherlock Holmes' nemesis, Moriarty, after a fellow pupil at Stonyhurst.*

2 Turn left before the farm and go through a wooden gate, following the line of the farm buildings to emerge onto a track. Keep straight ahead, following the hedge for 400m to reach the road. At the road, head right for 150m then take the lane on the left and follow this for 600m to reach **Hodder Place**. Beyond the residences, turn right to descend steeply and join the path alongside the **River Hodder**. Follow the river as the path becomes a track and joins the road.

3 At **Lower Hodder Bridge**, cross the road with care and head left on the bridge to admire Cromwell's Bridge which can be seen downstream (no public access). Follow the road uphill for 300m, then opposite the bus shelter, head left over the stile and climb along the field boundary to the brow of the hill above the woodland. Veer right over the field and through a kissing gate, heading for another kissing gate in the hedge and turn left along the tarmac track to **Winckley Hall**.

4 Descend the track and go left past the pond into the farmyard. Continue through the yard, turning left then right through a gate onto the track alongside the **River Hodder**. Continue past the confluence of the Hodder and Ribble, go over the stile beside the bench and join the track beside the **River Ribble** to a second confluence with the River Calder.

5 Continue for another 600m then go through a gate onto a track heading briefly away from the river before veering left to rejoin the river again. Continue alongside the River Ribble for another 1.2km, skirting the **aqueduct**. Head slightly right over the field and over a stile on the edge of the woodland to a footbridge.

6 Cross the wooden bridge, climb the steps and over another stile, following the fence on the left. Then continue across two bridges and another stile to emerge from the woodland and start climbing through the pasture along the left-hand field boundary. At the top of the field, head over the stile into the car park of the **Shireburn Arms** and cross the road back to your starting point.

WALK 4 – THE TOLKIEN TRAIL

Cromwell's Bridge over the River Hodder

Cromwell's crossing

Cromwell's Bridge – marked on the OS map as 'Old Bridge' – is named after the famous Civil War commander who is said to have led his 9000-strong New Model Army over this narrow packhorse bridge en route for the Battle of Preston. Cromwell did indeed stay at Stonyhurst during the Civil War, where he is said to have slept in his suit of armour for fear of assassination, but it's more likely that his army either forded the river or crossed one of the more substantial bridges upstream.

The footbridge over the railway at Mytton Fold

WALK 5
Dean Clough Reservoir

Start/finish	*Langho railway station*
Locate	*///dignitary.reward.arts*
Cafes/pubs	*Pub in York village*
Transport	*Trains from Clitheroe or Blackburn. Bus service 25 from Blackburn or Clitheroe*
Parking	*Limited on-street parking*
Toilets	*No public toilets on route*

Time 2hr
Distance 7km (4¼ miles)
Climb 190m

Follow in the footsteps of famous guidebook writer Alfred Wainwright on his youthful explorations of the countryside of the Ribble Valley

It was the view of Pendle Hill brooding on the horizon above Dean Clough Reservoir that first inspired a youthful Alfred Wainwright to venture from his home in Blackburn and further into the hills. After a steep initial climb from the station, this lovely walk offers expansive views over the Ribble Valley. Wainwright later described this view as 'a little piece of Lakeland in Lancashire'.

Looking south-west over the reservoirs

SHORT WALKS RIBBLE VALLEY

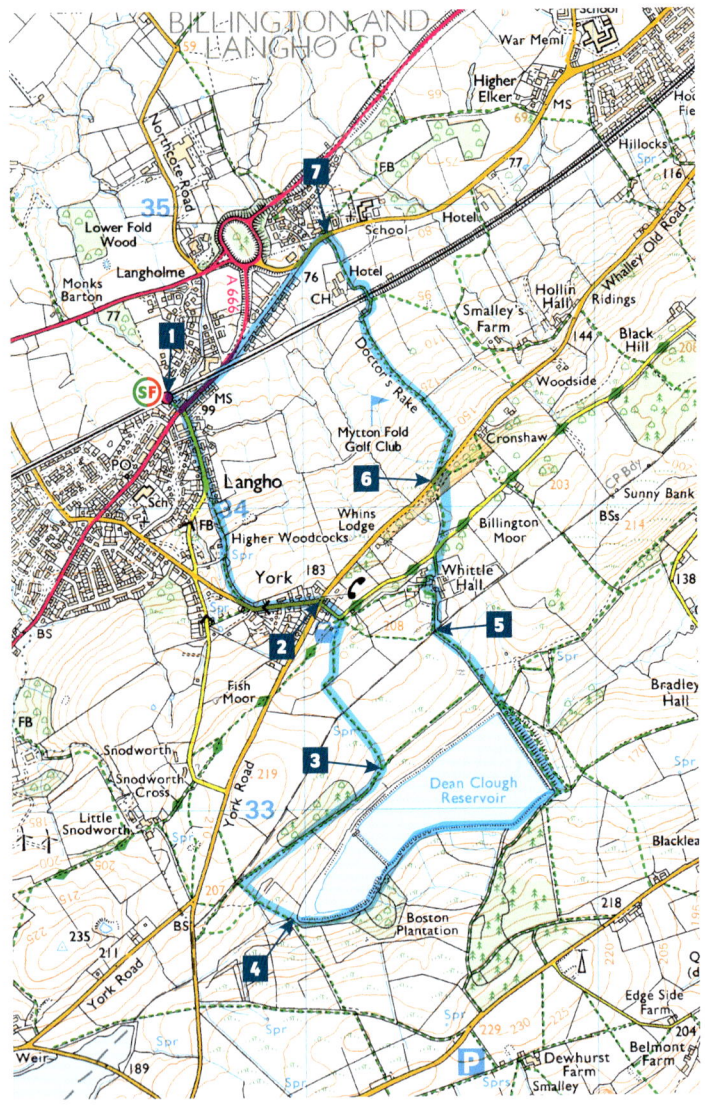

WALK 5 – DEAN CLOUGH RESERVOIR

1 From **Langho station**, head uphill to the main road, cross at the zebra crossing and continue up Whinney Lane. After 300m, where the lane forks right, take the footpath on the left, climbing steeply through the woods. Continue along the narrow path between residential gardens for 400m to reach the village of **York** and continue left up the lane to reach a crossroads. As you climb through the village, the views open up north to offer glimpses of the Bowland Fells, up the valley to Pendle and across the border into Yorkshire.

2 Head straight over past the postbox and continue climbing up the lane. After 100m, where the lane heads left, cross a stile and follow the right-hand path heading diagonally across the ridge towards the solitary tree, then join the drystone wall heading right to a stile. Cross the stile and head straight across the field. Go over the next stile and descend straight ahead towards **Dean Clough Reservoir** and reach a track.

3 Head right along the track to start a wide loop around the reservoir.

Dean Clough Reservoir seen from the woods above the north-western shoreline

37

View from the head (western end) of the reservoir looking north-east up to Pendle

Beyond the woods to the right, above the western end of the reservoir, join the path left, heading downhill to reach a kissing gate. Go through the kissing gate and then left through another gate onto the path around the reservoir.

4 Continue around the reservoir, past the wood and the causeway to the south-eastern corner, then head left across the dam. At the end of the dam, continue straight ahead, climbing the stony track beside the wall for 400m to reach a metal gate.

5 Through the metal gate, continue to the right of the rocky outcrop into the yard at **Whittle Hall**, and walk along the drive to cross the road. Take the lane on the left and descend over the field and through the woods to reach a road. Head briefly left and cross the road with care, then go through a wooden gate onto **Mytton Fold Golf Course**.

6 Join a gravel path as it threads its way between the fairways, then head downhill, following the black-and-white marker posts to cross the railway bridge, and continue past the hotel to the road.

7 Head left on the pavement, keeping left past the houses to rejoin the main A666 road and continue under the railway bridge back to **Langho station**.

– To shorten

To avoid the steep initial ascent and shave a couple of kilometres off the walk, there is limited parking on the street in York after Waypoint 2, beside the stile where the lane heads left. Follow the route as far as Waypoint 5, then cut left across the field to return to your starting point at the stile. This saves 3km (45 min).

Whalley Nab from beside the River Calder upstream of Whalley

WALK 6
Spring Wood and Whalley Nab

Start/finish	*Spring Wood, Whalley*
Locate	*///straddled.pinches.haggis*
Cafes/pubs	*Lots of bars and cafes in Whalley*
Transport	*Train to Whalley station near Waypoint 6*
Parking	*Spring Wood pay-and-display car park (BB7 9DP)*
Toilets	*In car park*

This pleasant circular walk combines natural history with industrial heritage, passing not one, but two Victorian railway viaducts along the way. The route meanders through woodland and beside the River Calder before climbing steeply up the flanks of Whalley Nab then dropping into the village, where there are ample opportunities to refuel before returning to your starting point.

Time 2½hr
Distance 8km (5 miles)
Climb 260m

A delightful walk starting in woodland and following the River Calder before climbing Whalley Nab then returning via the bustling village of Whalley

Spring Wood is famous for its dense drifts of spring bluebells

SHORT WALKS RIBBLE VALLEY

WALK 6 – SPRING WOOD AND WHALLEY NAB

Spring Wood is one of the best places in the Ribble Valley to admire the spring flush of bluebells in April, when the understorey is carpeted with swathes of these fragrant mauve blooms.

1 From the car park at **Spring Wood**, head back towards the entrance at the main road then take the footpath left over the stile and onto the golf course along the edge of the woods. Beware of flying golf balls! Climb steadily for 200m then head left over the footbridge and climb to a stile at the edge of the woodland. Cross the stile and continue climbing along the right-hand field boundary to arrive at the copse at the top of the incline.

2 Head sharp right through a kissing gate and follow the line of yellow-capped marker posts heading diagonally downhill then veering half left to meet the lane. Head right over a stile and along the lane to join the main road briefly before taking the footpath on the left. Continue across the field and downhill and over two stiles into a larger field. Continue straight ahead on a faint grassy path and over another stile, descending to a farm track. Head left on the track then right along the lane and over **Read Old Bridge**.

3 Over the bridge, take the footpath on the right heading across the field to the end of the woodland. Continue straight ahead over the stile to join a

The River Calder below Cock Bridge

track and follow this along the edge of the woods to the tarmac driveway leading to **Read Hall**. Turn right and follow the driveway to the main road beside the gatehouse. Cross the busy road with care and continue down the track opposite. As you approach the garden centre, look left to see the Martholme Viaduct spanning the River Calder. Carry on along the track to another busy main road and cross with care.

4 Head over **Cock Bridge** and take a footpath on the right before the pub. Follow the grassy path downhill and over a footbridge and follow the marker posts downstream. Ford a stream and climb steeply above the trees. Follow the path around the lip of the valley and through a kissing gate, continuing straight ahead into woods then veering left and then right to descend through a kissing gate and over a footbridge. Follow the path alongside a fence and then, beside a gate on the right, head slightly left across the next field, climbing steadily to the corner.

5 In the corner of the field, cross the stream on a flagstone bridge and continue beside the stream for 200m before recrossing and going through a kissing gate on the right. Climb very steeply to the top right-hand corner of the field and go through a kissing gate, then turn right along the holloway (sunken lane) to join Dean Lane. Follow the lane through the hamlet of

The river meanders through a steep wooded gorge upstream of Whalley

WALK 6 – SPRING WOOD AND WHALLEY NAB

Whalley Arches viaduct seen from the road bridge over the Calder

Whalley Banks and briefly a path before joining an access track. After 50m, fork right onto a bridleway, then join the footpath running parallel, descending steeply to meet a road.

> Just upstream of the bridge at Whalley lies a weir where an Archimedes screw has been generating renewable electricity since 2014. The turbine produces some 345,000kWh each year – enough to meet the electricity needs of 83 households.

6 Turn right and cross the bridge into **Whalley**. At the far side of the bridge, take the first road on the right into Calder Vale between houses and onto the riverside path. Follow the path upstream and then left to join a road. Cross the road, turn right, then take the footpath on the left after 30m. Follow the grassy path through the field to a kissing gate and cross the dual carriageway at the traffic lights to return to **Spring Wood**.

The old track down to Wymondhouses with the Bowland Fells in the distance

WALK 7
Wiswell, Portfield Bar and the Nick of Pendle

Start/finish	*Phone box by Coronation Garden in centre of Wiswell*
Locate	*///chest.cleansed.dives*
Cafes/pubs	*Pub in Wiswell*
Transport	*No public transport*
Parking	*On street in Wiswell*
Toilets	*No public toilets on route*

Time 2½hr
Distance 8km (5 miles)
Climb 205m

From the pretty village of Wiswell, this walk climbs past the site of an Iron Age hill fort and up to the Nick of Pendle

This short but rugged circular walk passes the site once occupied by an Iron Age hill fort and passes close to the mysterious grave of a medieval robber executed in the 14th century and buried outside the parish boundaries. Looping back via the Nick of Pendle to Wiswell, you'll have worked up an appetite for an indulgent lunch at The Freemasons, one of the Ribble Valley's best gastropubs.

Whalley Nab from near Clerk Hill

SHORT WALKS RIBBLE VALLEY

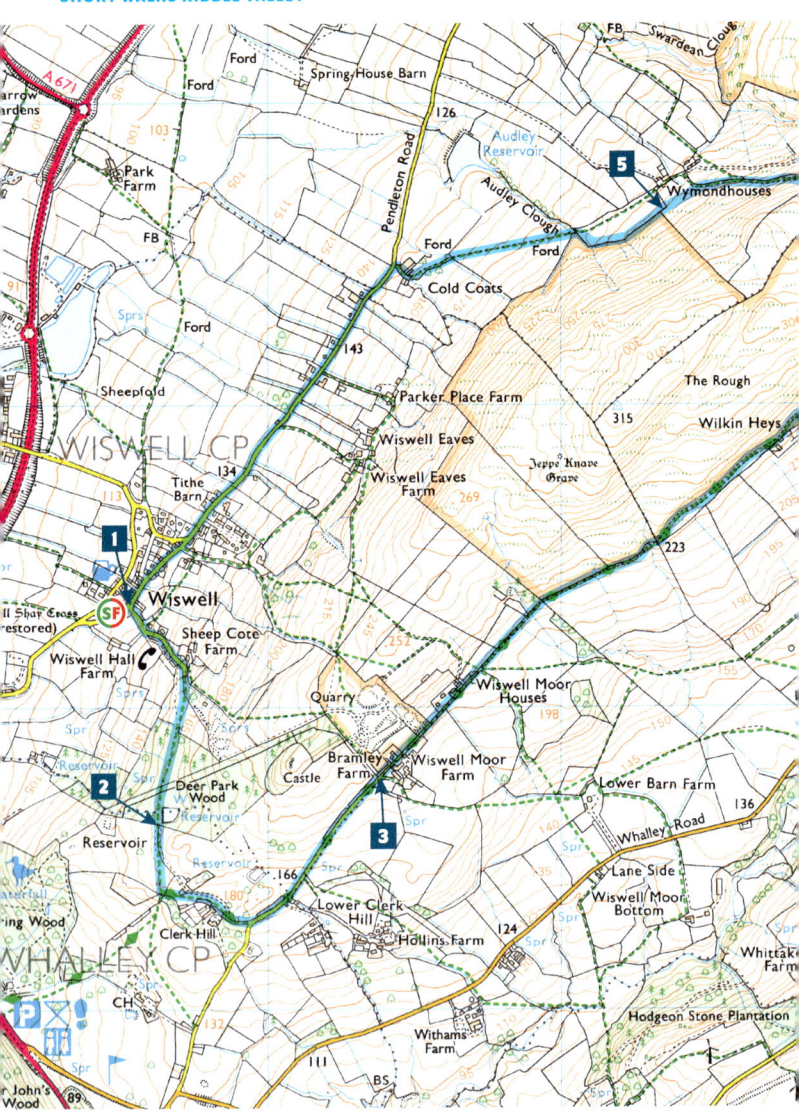

WALK 7 – WISWELL, PORTFIELD BAR AND THE NICK OF PENDLE

1 Park considerately on the roadside in the village and at the phone box at the crossroads in the village centre, head up Moor Lane, past the pumping station. Climb quite steeply up the lane and at **Sheep Cote Farm**, fork right through a gate and continue up the track and through another gate, then slightly left across the field and over the stile into **Deer Park Wood**. Head through the wood to a gate at the far side.

2 Leave the wood through the gate and continue straight ahead on a grassy track for 200m, then head right through a kissing gate and follow marker posts to a pair of kissing gates.

Pleasant dappled shade in Deer Park Wood

Go through the left-hand gate and follow the wall skirting **Clerk Hill**, then turn right over the stile onto a gravel track. Follow the track to a lane, turn left and follow the lane for 600m to **Bramley Farm**.

> At the south end of this ridge lies the faint earthworks of Portfield Bar hill fort, an Iron Age fortified farmstead. Unfortunately, there's no public access to the fort, but this – and other prehistoric earthworks hereabouts – suggest the ancient path you're following is at least 2500 years old.

3 Continue along the track past a string of farmhouses and through a gate, then stay on the track for 600m and go through a gate onto a grassy path veering slightly left. Follow the marker posts over the moorland to reach **Wilkin Heys** farmhouse. Continue along the track to the barn and onwards to the road. Head left alongside the road with care to reach the **Nick of Pendle**.

4 Stay on the left-hand side of the road and just beyond the Nick, take the stile on the left, descend the grassy track to a gate and cross over a stone stile. Continue descending diagonally on a track towards **Wymondhouses** farmhouse. Above the farmhouse, veer slightly left onto a faint path contouring above the barn to a metal gate.

> Just below the ridge up to your left is the grave of Jeppe the Knave, marked by an inscribed stone. Local robber Jeppe Curteys was buried here after his execution in 1327, adjacent to a Bronze Age burial site which may have been associated with the Portfield Bar hill fort.

The prehistoric remains of a burial cairn

WALK 7 – WISWELL, PORTFIELD BAR AND THE NICK OF PENDLE

The inscribed stone marking Jeppe the Knave's Grave

5 Go over the stone stile to the left of the gate and continue along the wall to the far end of the field, then head downhill and straight over the stile (ignore the second stile on the left), across the beck and up the other side of the ghyll. Continue diagonally across the next field, heading through the wide gap in the plantation towards the farmhouse at **Cold Coats**. In the corner of the field, go through a kissing gate and diagonally across the paddock to the farmhouse, then turn right through a gate and along the farm track to a lane. Turn left and walk 600m along the lane to return to **Wiswell** and the start.

> ⓘ *The Freemason's Arms at Wiswell is one of the Ribble Valley's premier gastropubs – featuring regularly in the UK's Top 50 restaurants.*

Looking back up to the trig point from the gravel path towards the shelter

WALK 8
The easy way up Pendle

Time 3hr
Distance 11km (6¾ miles)
Climb 300m

Start/finish	Nick of Pendle
Locate	///handlebar.cleanser.airless
Cafes/pubs	Pub near Nick of Pendle (300m off route)
Transport	No public transport
Parking	Limited parking at the Nick of Pendle (BB7 9HN)
Toilets	No public toilets on route

This route to the summit of Pendle Hill avoids the steep and sustained climb usually associated with Pendle and is an altogether easier undertaking

Pendle Hill dominates the entire Ribble Valley and is visible all the way from the sea to the source of the river above the iconic Ribblehead Viaduct. Steeped in myth and legend, Pendle is one of the most climbed hills in Lancashire, but reaching the summit usually involves a steep slog up the infamous 'Steps' from Barley. This route is altogether gentler, but it remains a fittingly rewarding challenge which feels like a proper hike!

The entire Pendle massif viewed from the south

1 Park in one of the informal car parks at the Nick of Pendle and cross the road with care to join the wide rutted track following the shallow ridge of **Apronful Hill**. Climb steadily and then more steeply for 2.5km, and after the track plateaus out then descends, take the path along the lip of **Ogden Clough**.

> Apronful Hill is so named because, according to local legend, the Devil dragged an apronful of rocks from the Deerstones Quarry to hurl at Clitheroe Castle – making the hole in the eastern flank of the keep with a direct hit.

2 Follow the path on the left side of the valley above the stream to the head of the clough. Cross the stream onto the summit plateau and follow the line of 'paving slabs' across the peat to the summit of **Pendle Hill**.

3 From the trig point at the **Big End** head north to the kissing gate beside the shelter then veer left through the gate, heading west on the 'ridge path' over the peat. This section can get boggy after heavy rain, so tread with care. Continue over the wall, along the edge of the plateau and past a shelter to reach a large memorial cairn.

> ⓘ *This route passes the Chartists' Well – an elusive trickle of water marking the site of a gathering of 2500 workers agitating for electoral reform in 1842.*

The section of the route between the kissing gate and the shelter occasionally affords a fleeting glimpse of the Central Lakeland Fells, peeping out in a shallow gap between the Bowland Fells away to the north.

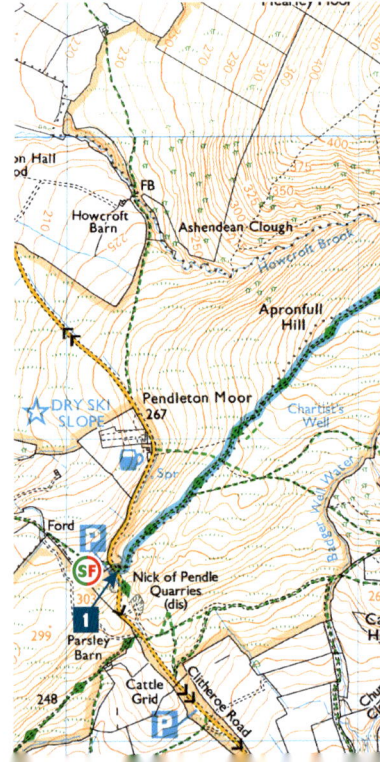

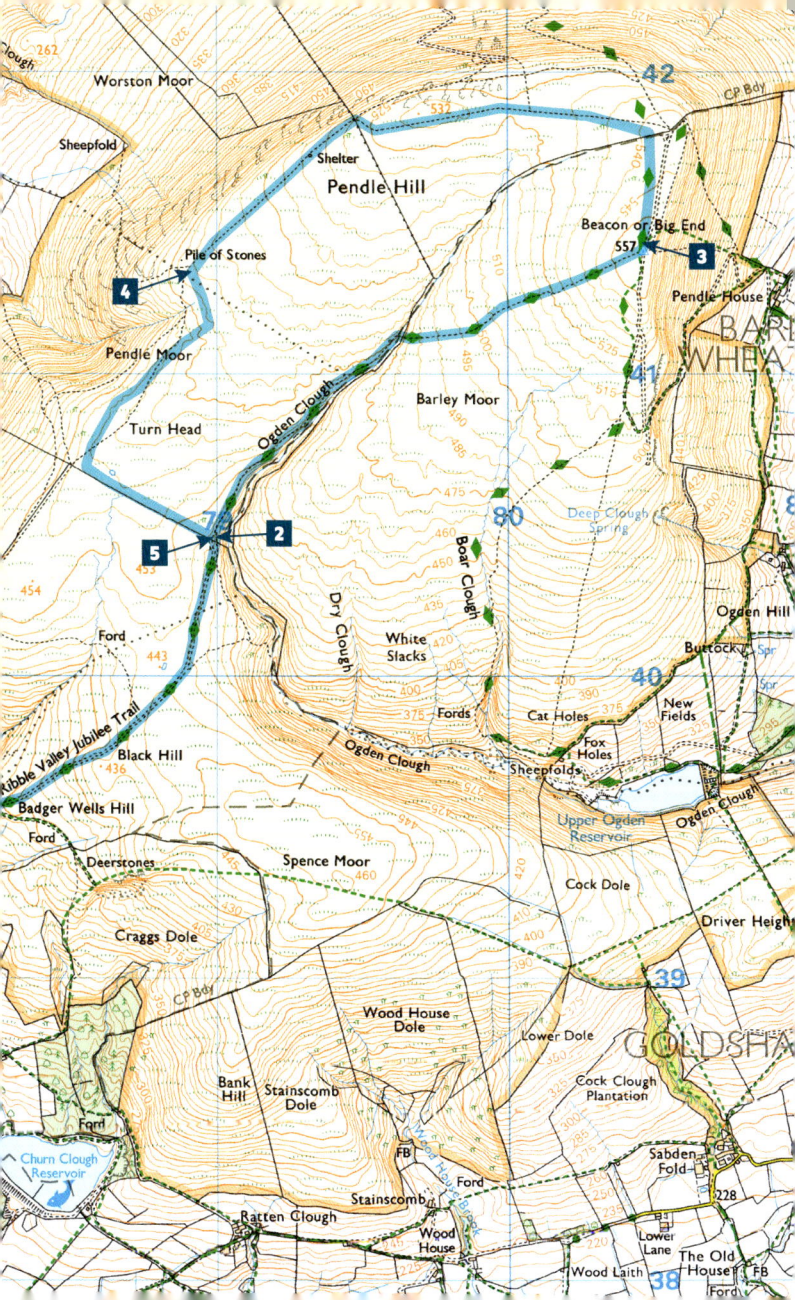

4 Continue along the edge of the plateau for another 600m on a section of improved footpath to reach a tumbledown wall. Follow this wall left for 500m to return to the footpath leading into **Ogden Clough**. Turn right and keep right. Do not follow the path forking left into the clough.

5 The right-hand path climbs gently to the summit of **Black Hill** from where you can retrace your steps to return to the **Nick of Pendle**. Cross the road with care back to the car park and your starting point.

Fox's Well – on the northern flank of the Big End – just below the summit plateau

The summit plateau on a spring morning

Fox's Well

In 1652, George Fox climbed Pendle Hill and upon reaching the 'Big End' – today marked by a trig point – he had a vision which inspired him to establish the Religious Society of Friends, better known as The Quakers. As he descended the hill, Fox drank from a well beneath the summit plateau, which is now marked by a plaque installed by the Pendle Radicals Project. The well is off route on a steep, unmade path and somewhat tricky to find.

Clitheroe Castle and grounds

WALK 9
Clitheroe Castle and the River Ribble

Start/finish	*Clitheroe railway station*
Locate	*///contain.diggers.automate*
Cafes/pubs	*Pubs and cafes in Clitheroe.*
Transport	*Hourly trains from Manchester and Blackburn. Buses from Burnley, Preston and Blackburn*
Parking	*Pay-and-display car parks at Chester Avenue (BB7 0ZZ) or Railway View (BB7 2EP)*
Toilets	*Railway View car park*

This easy walk is a pleasant 'town-into-country' route which explores Clitheroe's natural history and industrial heritage. Climb the ramparts of the Norman castle for expansive views of the surrounding countryside, then continue through a restored mill lodge at the heart of a green urban oasis.

Time 2hr
Distance 6.5km (4 miles)
Climb 75m

A fascinating circular walk via Clitheroe's historic castle, an urban nature reserve and the River Ribble

Primrose Community Nature Reserve

SHORT WALKS RIBBLE VALLEY

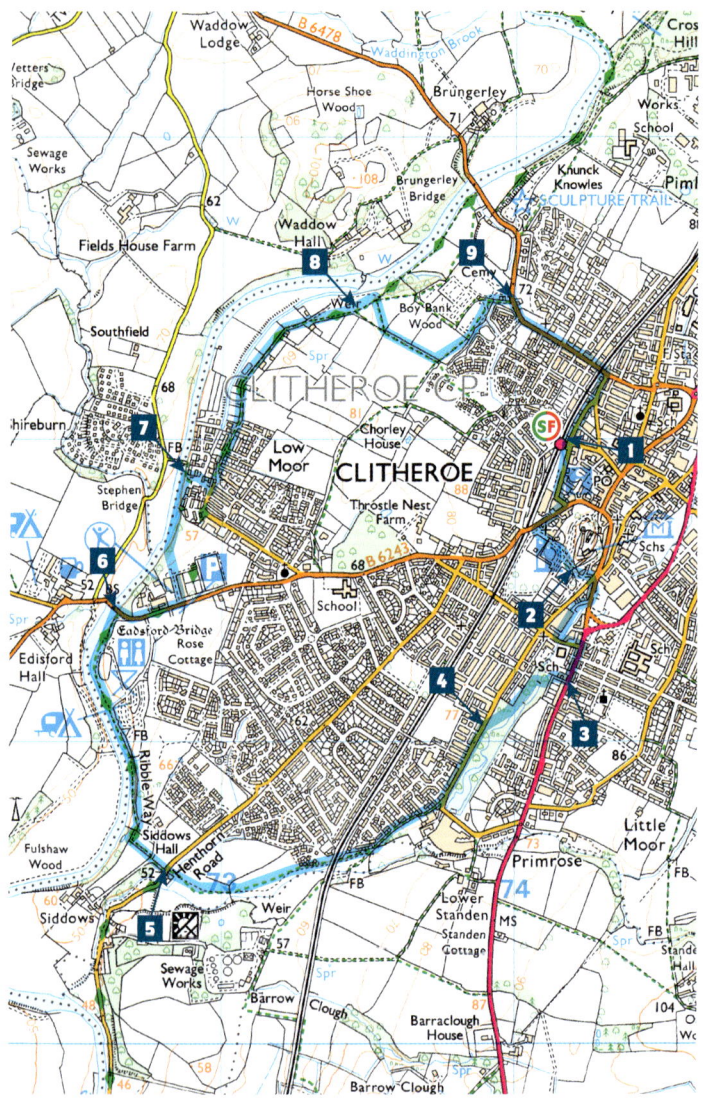

WALK 9 – CLITHEROE CASTLE AND THE RIVER RIBBLE

> ⓘ *The market town of Clitheroe is the administrative centre of the Ribble Valley and home to a host of pubs, cafes and independent retailers.*

The fish pass below the mill lodge

1 Turn right out of the **station** and continue past a supermarket, following the road round to the left. At the roundabout head right and veer slightly left into the **castle** grounds.

2 Explore the 11th-century keep then exit via the Woone Lane entrance, turning right after the Brown Cow pub and right again after 100m into the **Holmes Mill** complex. This historic cotton mill is now a retail and hospitality venue with cafes, bars, a deli and ice cream parlour. Continue through the complex and exit past the hotel onto **Greenacre Street**, heading left past the school then right along **Whalley Road**.

3 After 150m turn right down a cobbled lane between the pub and the Chinese restaurant and follow a path into the nature reserve. Cross a wooden bridge over Mearley Brook then follow the path left. Follow the walkway to exit on **Woone Lane** near the owl sculpture.

The Primrose Community Nature Reserve project restored the former mill lodge, removing thousands of tonnes of silt and rubbish and installing one of the UK's longest fish passes to allow Atlantic salmon to migrate up Mearley Brook after an absence of 200 years.

4 Head left along Woone Lane and where the road turns left, continue straight on along a tarmac driveway past the new apartment complex. Continue through a metal gate and follow the footpath into fields, under a

The weir on the River Ribble

railway bridge and alongside the brook across the fields to reach **Henthorn Road**.

5 Beside the houses, cross the road with care and follow the track on the far side round to the right then left, descending to the **River Ribble**. Follow the Ribble upstream for 800m to **Edisford Bridge**.

6 Head right on a footpath then cross Edisford Road at the pelican crossing and go along the drive past the swimming pool. Beyond the pool, follow a grassy path along the left-hand boundary of the field, briefly rejoining the river along the backs of the houses before heading right into the mill village of **Low Moor**.

> ⓘ *A disused mill in Clitheroe was used for secret testing of the first jet engine during WWII, before Rolls Royce in nearby Barnoldswick began commercial production.*

WALK 9 – CLITHEROE CASTLE AND THE RIVER RIBBLE

7 Continue over the roundabout, following the road right before cutting back left past the Old School and through the new housing estate, then onto a track past the allotments and stables to reach the **weir** after 500m.

8 Climb steeply up the slope above the weir to reach the marker post and head straight across the field to a gate. Go through the gate and along the left-hand field boundary. At far end of the field, head left through a kissing gate and across the field to join a footpath skirting the **cemetery**. Follow the path to Waddington Road.

9 Head right along the pavement, climbing briefly before descending towards the church spire. Continue under the railway bridge then turn right along Railway View Road for 200m to return to the **station**.

The pinnacle below the keep at Clitheroe Castle

Clitheroe Castle

A 12th-century Norman keep perched on a limestone knoll is all that remains of a much larger structure. Legend has it that the hole in the eastern wall was made by the Devil hurling rocks from the top of Pendle Hill, but it was more likely to have been a deliberate attempt to prevent the castle being used as a defensive structure during the Civil War. Admission to the castle and grounds is free, but there is a small admission charge for the adjacent Castle Museum.

Waddington Coronation Gardens

WALK 10
Waddington village circular

Start/finish	Waddington Arms, Waddington
Locate	///transmitted.round.recruiter
Cafes/pubs	Pubs in Waddington
Transport	Bus service 67 from Clitheroe
Parking	Behind the Waddington Arms (BB7 3HP)
Toilets	No public toilets on route

This easy circuit is an ideal route for a spring afternoon or a warm summer evening. Starting in the picturesque village of Waddington, the route heads through pastures and woodland, climbing gently onto the south-facing slopes of Waddington Fell and then returning to the village, where a cool pint awaits at one of Waddington's three excellent hostelries – the Waddington Arms, the Higher Buck and the Lower Buck Inn.

Time 2hr
Distance 7km (4¼ miles)
Climb 160m

A pleasant ramble through the pastures above Waddington and up onto the fell for extensive views before returning via pretty wooded ghylls

The Waddington Arms

SHORT WALKS RIBBLE VALLEY

WALK 10 – WADDINGTON VILLAGE CIRCULAR

1 From the front of the **Waddington Arms**, head over the bridge, past St Helen's Church and fork right at the Lower Buck Inn. After 50m turn right again up the driveway, go through a gate then left over the footbridge and over a stile. Continue along a path under the trees and over another stile, then head half left across the field. Go straight over the field to a stile, then go right through a gate to a stile under trees on the far side of the field.

2 Cross the stile and head right for 75m, then go left over the bridge and follow the path along the field boundary to a footbridge in a copse at the far side of the second field. Continue straight across the field in front of **Colthurst Hall** to a stile at the end of the wall. Go over the stile and turn left down the track, then go right over the first stile and right again across the field parallel to the boundary to reach a stile on the edge of the woods. Cross the stile and go through the dense woodland to a footbridge and onto **Cross Lane** – known by locally as Rabbit Lane. The ancient hedgerows and dense woodland alongside Rabbit Lane are a wonderful place to spot rare birds such as the redstart, pied flycatcher and redpoll.

3 Turn left and continue gently downhill along the lane for 150m then take the bridleway on the right. Continue climbing for 500m, jinking right then left and continuing along the edge of the wood and through a kissing gate. Continue slightly left along the perimeter of the woodland then along a wall and through two gates to the next wall. Turn right to follow the wall, then go through a gateway towards **Daisy Hill Farm**. The views from the lower slopes of Waddington Fell afford pleasing views across the Ribble Valley to Pendle Hill.

Waddington Fell

The woods at Whinney Lane

4 At the building, go over a stile and follow the path around to the right of the farm, then continue straight across fields for 250m, jinking right through a gate and following telegraph poles and over stiles to **Fell Road**.

5 Cross the road with caution into Mill Lane and continue straight on for 200m, then take the footpath right down a track signposted 'Tagglesmire Hall'. Continue downhill between the houses and into a wooded ghyll.

6 Cross a footbridge and climb steeply left then right to follow the path along the lip of the ghyll. Continue straight down through the fields and right of the irrigation **reservoir**, then go over the stile.

7 Walk through a farmyard then turn right down a faint path into the ghyll and left over a steep stone stile into a field. Continue descending through the fields beside the ghyll for 600m and as the church spire appears ahead, make for the line of sycamore trees and follow the track before joining the path past the almshouses back into the village. At the road, turn right then left down the lane back to the **Waddington Arms**.

WALK 11
Waddington and Bashall Eaves from Edisford

Time 2¾hr
Distance 9km (5½ miles)
Climb 120m

A walk through pastureland to the hamlet of Bashall Eaves and on to the picturesque village of Waddington before returning via the River Ribble

Start/finish	Car park on Edisford Road, Clitheroe
Locate	///existence.undertone.digests
Cafes/pubs	Pubs and cafes in Clitheroe and Waddington
Transport	Bus service 11 from Clitheroe
Parking	Edisford pay-and-display car park (BB7 3LA)
Toilets	Edisford riverside embankment

The riverside at Edisford Bridge has been a popular bathing spot since Victorian times and it has been a strategically important river crossing since the early medieval period. This route leaves the crowds of paddlers and picnickers behind and criss-crosses the old Lancashire–Yorkshire border country to arrive in Waddington with its three great pubs.

The Saddle Bridge at Bashall Eaves

SHORT WALKS RIBBLE VALLEY

1 From the car park, turn left and follow the pavement to cross the bridge and head up the road past the **Edisford Bridge Inn**. After the pub, head right at the junction, passing the entrance to the campsite, and take the footpath through the hedge on the right. Head towards the copse, over a stile and continue along the field boundary to the farm track. Go over the stiles and into the next field, passing left of the farm and descending to a stile in the hedge.

2 Cross the next field and go past the pumping station to find a stile under the pylons, then go over the track and past the copse to climb to a gate in the hedge on the far side.

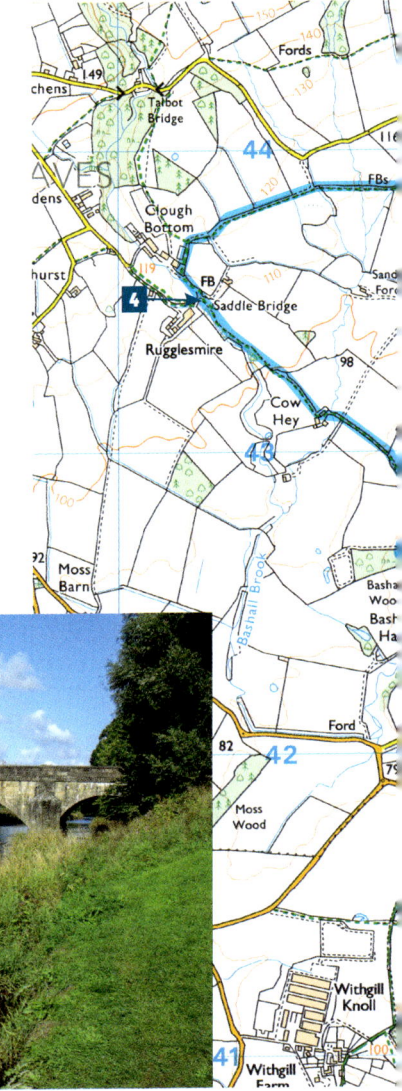

Edisford Bridge over the River Ribble

WALK 11 – WADDINGTON AND BASHALL EAVES FROM EDISFORD

3 Head left through the gate to cross Twitter Lane and take the faint footpath diagonally left across the field to join a track past **Bashall Hall**. Follow this track to Cow Hey Farm and look for a footpath on the right. Follow the path beside the stream up to **Saddle Bridge**.

> ⓘ *The Saddle Bridge – or Fairy Bridge – just outside the hamlet of Bashall Eaves is a Grade II listed structure.*

4 Continue past bridge and left into the lane for 75m before taking a path off to the right past the barns of **Clough Bottom** and around the copse to a stile. Cross the stile and go right along a gravel track for 300m to a cattle grid, then take the path down to the right. Ford the stream and head through the iron gate then follow the left-hand field boundary to cross two footbridges and reach a stile onto a driveway.

5 Head right over the stile, then left between the houses and right at the gate and through another gate into a narrow wooded path leading into open fields. At the end of the path, turn immediately left and follow the faint path along the field boundary to the yard at **Lower New House Farm**.

6 Go straight through the yard to the track at the far end and follow this track right and then left over the bridge. Continue through three gates and past the barn. Stay on the track

The Lower Buck Inn

Looking back towards Clitheroe and Pendle from Bashall Eaves

over the cattle grid and through the last gate and into **Waddington**.

Until 1974, the River Ribble formed the boundary between Lancashire and Yorkshire. This is reflected at the Lower Buck Inn, where the red rose of Lancashire and the white rose of Yorkshire adorn the stained-glass inner door.

7 Turn right after the Lower Buck Inn then straight on at the fork to join Edisford Road. Continue on this road for 1.5km, past **Shireburn Caravan Park**, then left over the footbridge and right into the former mill village of **Low Moor**.

8 Follow the riverside footpath along the backs of the houses and across the playing fields to join the road between the tennis courts and swimming pool. When you reach the main road, cross via the pedestrian crossing and return to the car park.

Footpath marker on the track up to Lane Head Barn

WALK 12
The foothills of Pendle from Downham

Start/finish	*Bridge on Main Street, Downham*
Locate	*///storming.foods.demoted*
Cafes/pubs	*Pub and cafe in Downham*
Transport	*Bus service 64 or 67 from Clitheroe*
Parking	*Village car park off Main Street (BB7 4BN)*
Toilets	*In car park*

The village of Downham comprises a cluster of pretty stone cottages, a church and a pub nestling in a secluded hollow below the summit of Pendle Hill. It's an idyllic location, which was chosen as the setting for a film and a TV series. This walk starts in the village and climbs gently among the foothills of Pendle.

Time 2½hr
Distance 8km (5 miles)
Climb 250m

This scenic hike from the picture-postcard village of Downham makes the perfect prelude to a hearty lunch or indulgent dinner at the pub

Stunning views up the Ribble Valley to the Yorkshire Three Peaks

The idyllic village of Downham

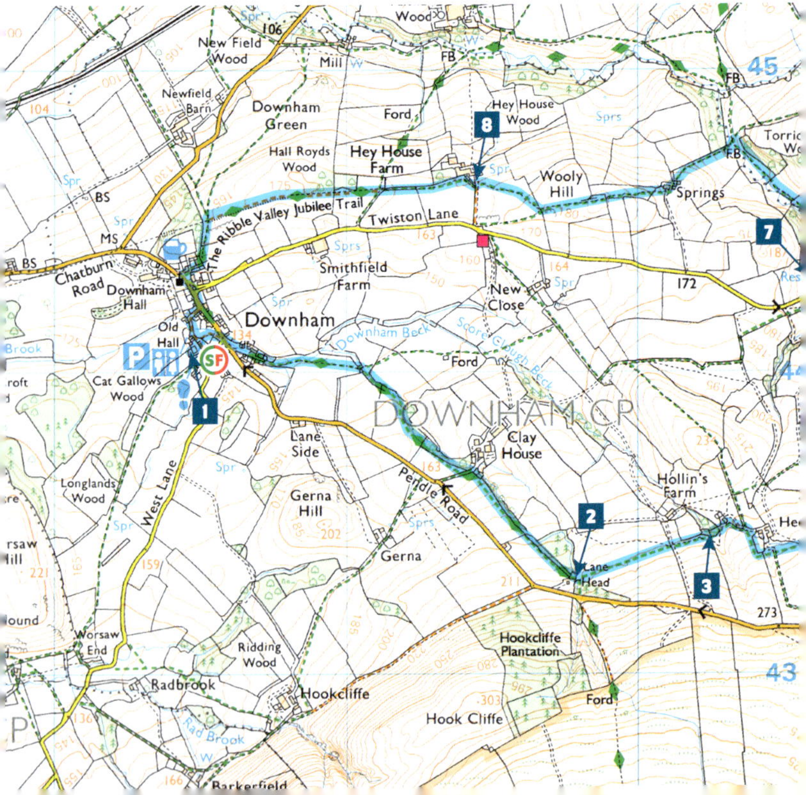

WALK 12 – THE FOOTHILLS OF PENDLE FROM DOWNHAM

1 From the bridge at the centre of the village, follow the beck upstream and along the lane, then cross a footbridge and follow Town End Road onto the footpath. Follow the path beside the stream, then go half right to the top corner of the field. Climb alongside the fence and over a footbridge. Continue straight over the track and along the field boundary to **Lane Head barn**.

2 Head left across the stream and straight over the fields, keeping the marker posts to your left. Cross the stone stile, continuing straight over the track and along the edge of the field then over the stile in the corner of the field beside the copse.

3 Head towards the farm buildings. Keep right of the first farm, following the boundary wall to a narrow stone stile. Crossing the stile, continue over the track, following the marker stone to another stile. Follow the field boundary past the next farmhouse, then turn left on the track uphill for 75m before descending half left along the edge of the field and into the wooded ghyll.

4 Continue over the footbridge and climb through a kissing gate and steeply up across the field, passing the barn, then go over a footbridge before climbing up to a cottage.

5 Turn left and over a stile and follow the fence along the right-hand field boundary. Go through a gate then over a squeeze stile, following the hedge on your left to a stile in the bottom corner of the field. Cross the stile, then follow the hedge right and go through the gate, then head half left across the next field and through the squeeze stile. Cross the field to a gate left of the farm and go over the stile.

77

Rolling pastureland above Twiston

6 Follow the field edge to a gate then drop down into the ghyll and past the barn. Ignore a footbridge on your left and head for a kissing gate in the corner of the field, then follow the stream and turn right through a gate onto a quiet lane.

> ⓘ *The Assheton Arms in Downham was transformed into the Signalman's Arms at the heart of the fictional village of Ormston in the BBC Drama Born and Bred.*

7 Continue along the lane for 150m, then take the footpath on the left beside **Twiston Mill** and follow the path downstream beside the beck through kissing gates and left over the footbridge. Follow the wall to the cottage, go through the gates between the buildings and turn right over the stile. Continue to the tree at the top of **Wooly Hill** and over the stile. Continue straight ahead to the next stile then bear half right towards the buildings.

8 Go straight over the track and continue along the edge of fields then along the edge of woodlands and across a field, before taking the footpath left and joining the lane to the **Assheton Arms**. Opposite the church, descend steeply down the lane back to the starting point at the bridge.

The idyllic village of Downham was the setting for the 1961 film *Whistle Down the Wind*, starring a youthful Hayley Mills alongside children from the village school. More recently, Downham became the fictitious village of Ormston in the BBC drama *Born and Bred*.

WALK 13
Grindleton Fell and the pine woods

Time 3¼hr
Distance 10km (6¼ miles)
Climb 325m

A varied walk from the charming village of Grindleton through farmland and coniferous forest to a lofty viewpoint

Start/finish	The Rum Fox, Grindleton
Locate	///powering.sourced.divisible
Cafes/pubs	Pub at Grindleton
Transport	Bus service 66 or 67 from Clitheroe
Parking	Limited on-street parking in the village
Toilets	No public toilets on route

One of the Ribble Valley's best-kept secrets, this is one of the more challenging hikes in this collection, but it's well worth the effort. Leaving the handsome stone village of Grindleton, the route climbs almost constantly for more than an hour and a half, but the views and the return journey through dense pine woods make this a memorable mini-expedition. Take your time on the steeper ascents and pack some drinks and snacks to keep your energy levels up.

Memorial stone and seating area in Grindleton

SHORT WALKS RIBBLE VALLEY

Grindleton is mentioned in the Domesday Book and is an example of a Saxon planned village which later became associated with jam-making and bee-keeping – reflected in the church being dedicated to St Ambrose, patron saint of beekeepers.

1 From **The Rum Fox** pub in the centre of the village, cross the road with care and head north up **Main Street**, climbing steadily through the village and forking left after 500m onto Whitehall Lane. Follow the lane to the **White Hall** itself, and take the bridleway opposite on the right, continuing to climb steadily past **Cob Manor** and into open country to the end of the track.

2 Go through the gate at the end of the track and follow the wall on the left of the grassy path to the next gate, then veer slightly left and climb steeply on another grassy path to a lane.

3 Head left and follow the lane along the edge of the plantation. After 800m, follow the track round to the right,

The road from Grindleton up to the Pinewoods plantation

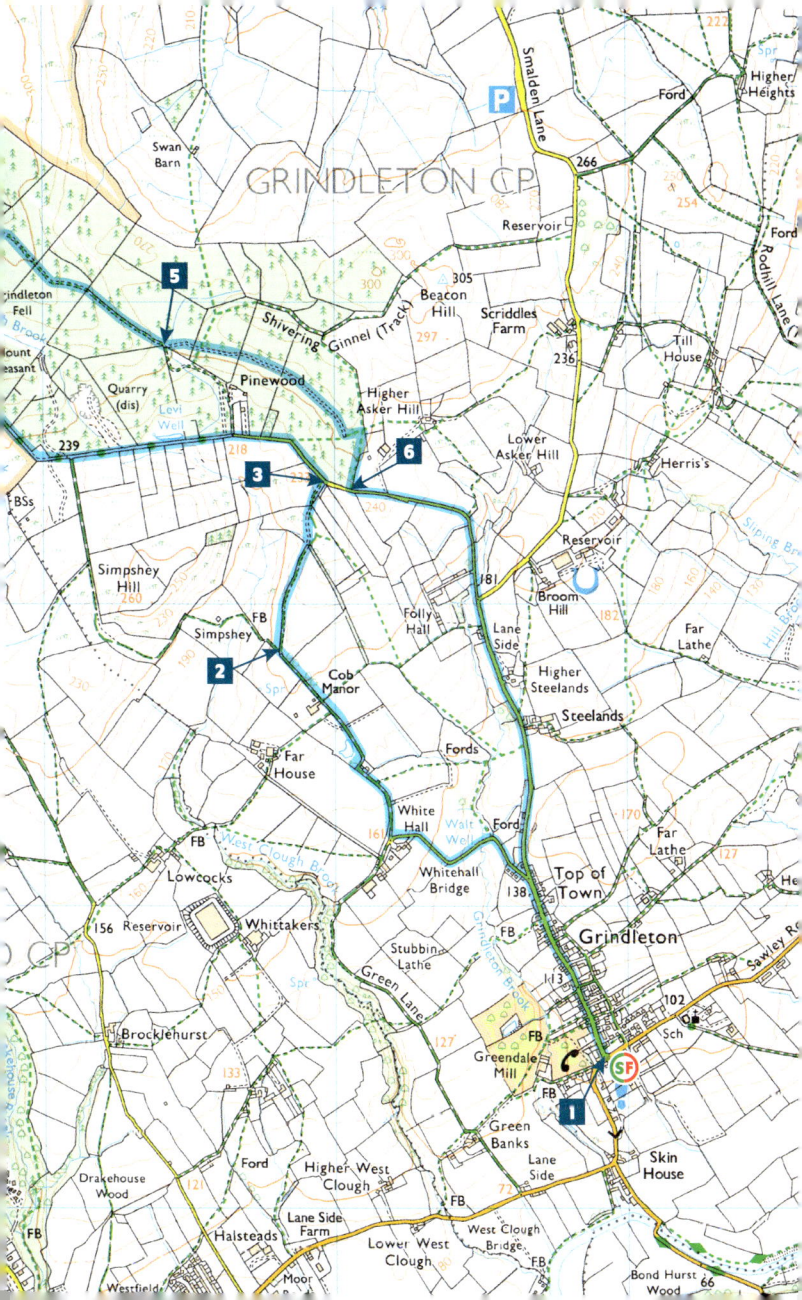

climbing more steeply through two gates to the top of the plantation, then heading slightly left to reach the cairn up on the skyline near the summit of **Bradford Fell**. From the cairn there are outstanding views over the Ribble Valley to Pendle.

4 From the cairn, head right and descend steadily beside the wall at the edge of the trees and through a gate. Continue into the pines along an often-muddy firebreak, joining an eroded path heading left then dropping steeply right into a clearing. Cross the beck and continue descending more steadily to join a rocky track and follow it for 700m to a fork.

5 Where the main track heads right, continue straight ahead on a narrow path through the trees. Follow the footpath as it meanders through the trees for 500m then joins a footpath heading right along the edge of the plantation. Follow this path to the lane.

6 Head left, following the road downhill and round to the right before joining the main road to return to your starting point in **Grindleton**.

> **− To shorten**
>
> To miss out the climb from Grindleton, park considerately in one of the informal laybys on the quiet lane near Waypoint 3 and follow the directions from there, turning right when you return to the lane at Waypoint 6. This shortens the walk by just under 5km (1hr 25min) and halves the amount of ascent (170m).

Views to Pendle from the summit of Bradford Fell (Walk 13)

WALK 14
Sawley and Bolton-by-Bowland

Start/finish *Spread Eagle Inn, Sawley*
Locate *///riders.compress.travels*
Cafes/pubs *Pub in Sawley, cafe in Holden, pub in Bolton-by-Bowland*
Transport *Bus service C3 or 280 from Clitheroe*
Parking *On roadside in Sawley*
Toilets *Bolton-by-Bowland public car park*

Time 2½hr
Distance 9.5km (6 miles)
Climb 210m

A steep climb up an ancient holloway, followed by a gentle descent into Bolton-by-Bowland before returning via the River Ribble to Sawley

This is quite a rugged walk, with a steep climb up an ancient holloway (sunken lane) to an elevated viewpoint before a gentle descent into the historic village of Bolton-by-Bowland. The return is through the parkland of Bolton Hall – one-time refuge of King Henry VI after his defeat during the Wars of the Roses.

Bijou accommodation beside Rodhill Lane

Pendle seen from near the top of Rodhill Lane

1 From the Spread Eagle Inn in **Sawley**, follow the road round to cross the bridge over the **River Ribble**, keeping left at the junction then right up the first tarmac driveway. At the end of the driveway, head straight ahead up a block-paved drive and go left of the garage into the wood, then right through a kissing gate into a field. Head across the field to the right of a large tree and continue through a metal gate in the corner of the field and go half left along the track towards a farmhouse. At the farmhouse, go left through the two gates, following the field boundary for 40m, then turn right through another gate.

2 Cross the field staying parallel to the right-hand field boundary and go through the metal gate then across the paddock and through the gate in the right-hand corner into woodland, descending to cross the footbridge. Climb the bank on the far side and follow the left-hand field boundary, then go left through a metal gate, continuing along the other side of the field boundary towards woodland. At a driveway, either follow the track as it zigzags up to the cottage or follow the bridleway left through the copse to reach **Rodhill Gate**.

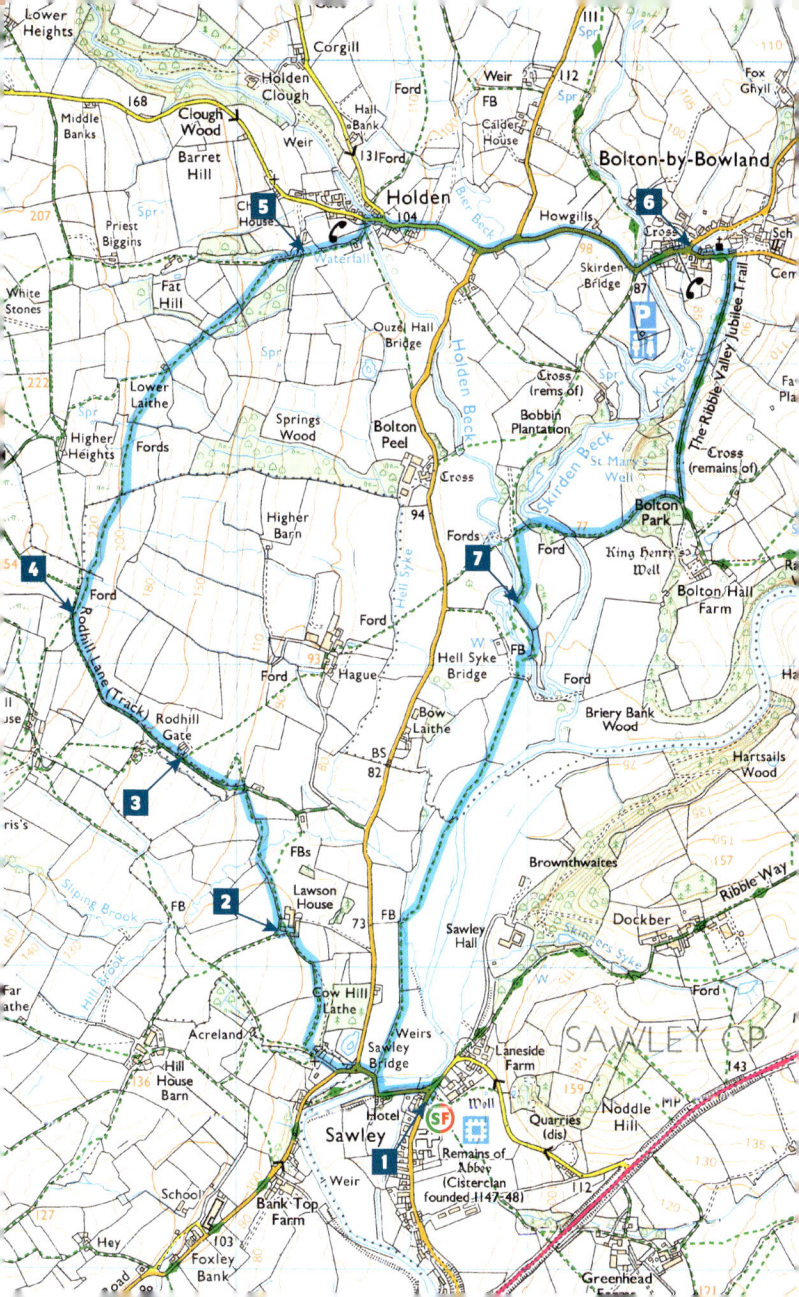

Bolton-by-Bowland village green

3 Continue climbing up the track then go through the gate and onto **Rodhill Lane**. This ancient holloway can be tricky underfoot, so take care for the next 400m or so. Continue through two gates as the track steepens, and at the top of the track, as you emerge from the tree cover, keep to the right-hand side of the path and look for a stile on the right at the apex of the fence corner.

4 Cross the stile and follow the left-hand field boundary to cross another stile, then veer slightly right across the next field, through a gate, over the next field and through another gate. Head for the barn and go through the stone stile, then head half left across the field and through the gate. Go straight down the field and over the stile then through a gate. Head downhill through a gap in the hedge and continue to the stone stile in the bottom left-hand corner of the field. Tread quietly through the next field and you may see the resident herd of deer hiding in the plantation on the right.

5 Go over the stone stile then over a track to cross the next stone stile and head straight across the field to a wooden gate. Walk between hedges and past a house onto a track into the village of **Holden**. Head right over the bridge past the postbox, then right again. Walk along the road with care, heading left at the junction, over the bridge then straight on for 300m and over the bridge into the village of **Bolton-by-Bowland**, with a village

WALK 14 – SAWLEY AND BOLTON-BY-BOWLAND

The Coach & Horses at Bolton-by-Bowland

green complete with stocks and a whipping post.

6 Continue past the Coach and Horses pub and St Peter and St Paul's Church and head right along the driveway between the avenue of trees that leads to **Bolton Hall**.

Following his defeat by the Yorkists at the Battle of Hexham in 1464, King Henry VI was sheltered by Ralph Pudsey at Bolton Hall, where a well is named after him.

After 800m, at the cattle grid, turn right along a gravel track and follow it through fields to the river. Cross the river on a footbridge and follow the track past a copse then, at gateposts, take the footpath on the left following the field boundary next to the river and continue through the gate.

7 Follow the fence line above the flood meadows for 200m and go over a footbridge over the **Skirden Beck**. Go straight across the meadow to a kissing gate and follow the grassy path through the fields for 700m, veering gently right to cross the beck, then along the hedge to the **Sawley Bridge**. Cross the bridge and head left along the road to return to your starting point.

The bridge over the Ribble at Sawley

The River Ribble in spate at Sawley

WALK 15
Sawley to Clitheroe along the Ribble Way

Start	*The Spread Eagle Inn, Sawley*
Finish	*Clitheroe Interchange, Railway View Road*
Locate	*///riders.compress.travels*
Cafes/pubs	*Plenty of options in Clitheroe, pub in Sawley*
Transport	*Bus service C3 or 280 from Clitheroe*
Parking	*Railway View Avenue pay-and-display car park, Clitheroe (BB7 2EP)*
Toilets	*On lane adjacent to car park*

Time 2½hr
Distance 9km (5½ miles)
Climb 100m

This flat, linear walk follows the meandering course of the River Ribble via the villages of Grindleton and West Bradford

The Ribble Way stretches for more than 100km from the Yorkshire Dales to the Fylde Coast, but this short section makes an easy afternoon hike with good public transport connections between start and finish. It's a flat and peaceful riverside ramble through pastures and woodland with kingfishers, squirrels and perhaps even the glimpse of an otter along the way. To reach the start catch the 280 or C3 bus from Clitheroe Interchange to Sawley.

Ribble Way signage

SHORT WALKS RIBBLE VALLEY

The Spread Eagle Inn in Sawley

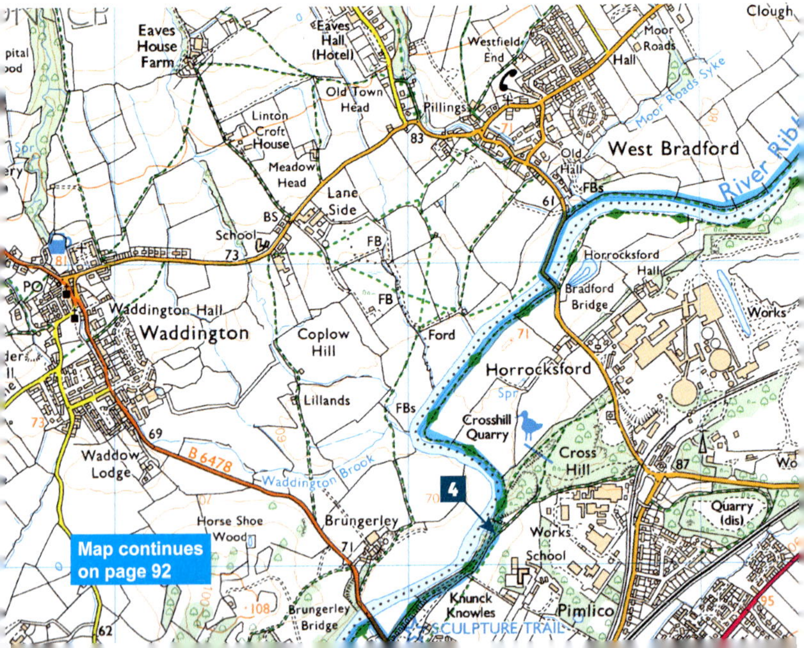

1 Before setting off, the remains of Sawley Abbey are just a short walk from the pub and entry is free. From the Spread Eagle Inn in **Sawley**, follow the road beside the river downstream and cross the bridge, taking the riverside footpath on the left on the far side of the bridge. Follow the path downstream and rejoin the road for 500m, climbing steeply and passing **Bowland High School**, then take the footpath over the stone stile on the left.

2 Follow the faint path downhill to a stile in the bottom right-hand corner of

SHORT WALKS RIBBLE VALLEY

> ⓘ *The Ribble Valley was an important strategic route for pre-historic nomadic tribes, Romans and Vikings – evidenced by arte-facts like the Cuerdale Hoard of Viking Silver found in 1840.*

the field and continue downhill and through a kissing gate, then over the flood meadows and through another kissing gate to join the riverside path heading downstream. Follow the river for 700m, and after the road bridge, head left through a kissing gate to join the road and continue past the ter-raced houses on the left to the road junction.

3 Turn left and almost immediately left again along Ribble Lane past the houses and go through a gate to the **River Ribble**. Continue downstream for 1.5km past the water treatment

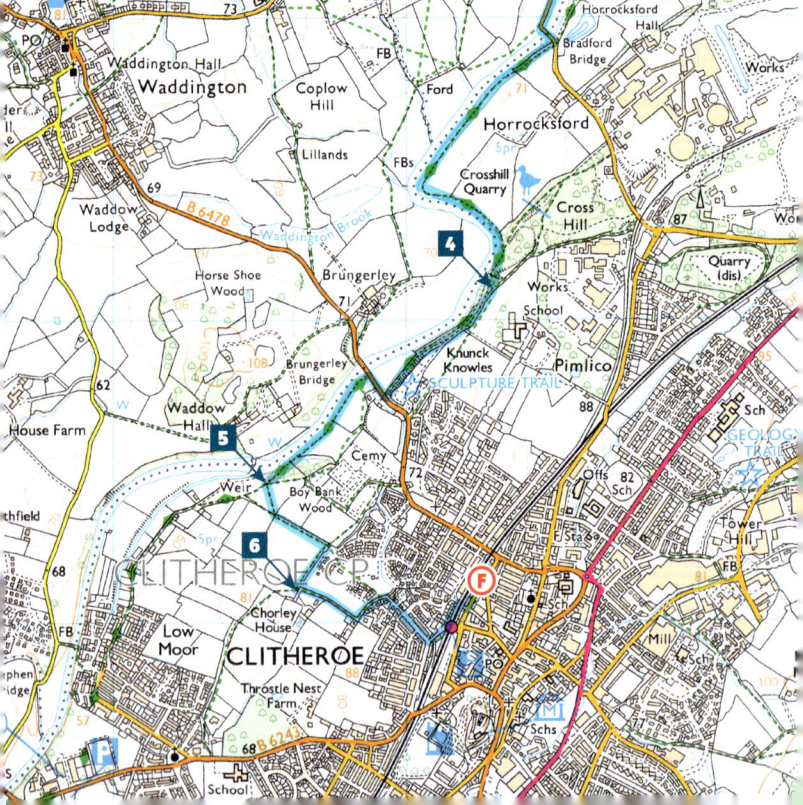

works and over three footbridges to reach the road on the edge of the village of **West Bradford**. Follow the road across the bridge and on the far side, take the riverside footpath on the right and continue downstream for 500m, following the river round a sharp bend and through a kissing gate into **Crosshill Quarry Nature Reserve**.

> Opened in 1993, the Ribble Valley Sculpture Trail was the first in the country, featuring 20 works of art among the woodlands of Crosshill Quarry Nature Reserve. Sculptures alongside the riverside footpaths depict the wildflowers and wildlife to be found in the reserve.

4 Turn right at the otter sculpture onto the gravel path and after 200m, veer left up the steep tarmac ramp to join the upper path through the woods, After another 200m, fork right to rejoin the lower path and emerge on the road approaching **Brungerley Bridge**. Cross the road with care, and before the bridge, take the footpath left down the steep steps. Continue downstream on a grassy riverside path through the woods to the **weir**.

5 After admiring the weir, head uphill away from the river to join a footpath heading through a gate and into the next field. Follow the left-hand field boundary and at the far end of the field, follow the hedge right along the field boundary then left through a kissing gate and immediately left through another kissing gate onto a gravel track.

6 Follow the track around the edge of the new housing development to join Kirkmoor Road in **Clitheroe**. Continue towards the castle then, at the end of the road, head left through the sheltered accommodation and onto the footpath past the back of the railway station then right under the bridge and left to return to the interchange.

Ottter in the Sculpture Trail in Crosshill Quarry Nature Reserve

Sawley Abbey

Sawley Abbey

Founded in 1146, Sawley Abbey was eclipsed by the establishment, a century and a half later, of the larger Whalley Abbey, 14.5km away (see Walk 6). In 1536, the monks fled the Abbey in the face of Henry VIII's onslaught against the monasteries, but briefly returned during the Pilgrimage of Grace (a rebellion against Henry VIII and the English Reformation) under a new Abbot, James Trafford. The 'Pilgrimage' fizzled out the following year and Trafford was hanged at Lancaster. The Abbey was abandoned and plundered for its valuables and stone, which was reused in neighbouring farms and cottages. The Abbey is owned by English Heritage and entry is free.

USEFUL INFORMATION

Tourism bodies

Visit Lancashire www.visitlancashire.com

Visit Ribble Valley www.visitribblevalley.co.uk

Tourist information centres

Station Road, Clitheroe

Travel

Bus

Bus timetables www.lancashire.gov.uk

For bus information for your chosen stop direct to your mobile phone www.nextbuses.mobi

Rail

Northern www.northernrailway.co.uk

Traveline www.traveline.info tel 0871 200 22 33

Text info: 84268 (for live bus timetable information)

© Mark Sutcliffe 2025
First edition 2025
ISBN: 978 1 78631 236 5
eISBN: 978 1 78765 150 0

Printed in Singapore by KHL Printing using responsibly sourced paper.
A catalogue record for this book is available from the British Library.
All photographs are by the author unless otherwise stated.
Cover illustration of Cromwell's Bridge by John Bingley.

© Crown copyright and database rights 2025 OS AC0000810376

CICERONE

Cicerone Press, Juniper House, Murley Moss, Oxenholme Road,
Kendal, Cumbria, LA9 7RL

www.cicerone.co.uk

Updates to this Guide

While every effort is made to ensure the accuracy of guidebooks as they go to print, changes can occur during the lifetime of an edition. Any updates that we know of for this guide will be on the Cicerone website (www.cicerone.co.uk/1236/updates), so please check before planning your trip. We also advise that you check information about transport, accommodation and shops locally. Even rights of way can be altered over time. We are always grateful for information about any discrepancies between a guidebook and the facts on the ground, sent by email to updates@cicerone.co.uk.

Register your book: To sign up to receive free updates, special offers and GPX files where available, create a Cicerone account and register your purchase via the 'My Account' tab at www.cicerone.co.uk.